THE SHAPE
OF
MY LOVE

SANDEEP DAHIYA

The Shape of My Love

The sage dispelling haze

Lynched by life's rage,
All puzzled, shaky and
in the grip of debilitating daze,
I run around
and seek the help of a sage
living in a hut in the hills
where many throng to get spiritual pills
after failures with materialistic bills.

The ascetic is all joy,
Says, come my beaten, bruised boy,
I tell him the story of my woes,
Show him the empty rows
where I planted loving, caring seeds,
But 'their'—the others—unfaithful deeds
undid my loving labor's creeds.

Seeing me all lost,
smiled the kind host,
Gently he took me to a place,
Aha, paradise in full embrace,
Such a heavenly brace,
Trees, hills and sky's blue,—
nature's pristine hue,
The beauty was spread out there
like an otherworldly layer,
Joyfully lit my eyes
far away from painful cries.

Then he pinched my earlobe,
Winced I with pain and sob,
The beauty instantly vanished,
All joy banished,

Though it was there still,
But I lost it due to the bitter pill.

Says the kindly sage,
dispelling my illusions and haze:
'Other people and situations just are
as they are here and far,
We are primarily at war
with our self own,
The seeds that are sown
within our own self
decide fruits, crops and pelf.

Gently reminds me the sage,
softly turning wisdom's page,
'Long before others cause us pain,
the prickly seed has already lain
within us for a long time,
The externals merely chime
with the seed's potential prime,
How will you get sweetness from a lime?'

Lonely trees

These are lonely trees,
Alone and forlorn,
Standing as the last fighting units
of the defeated forest army,
Their long and broad
robust columns of soldiers gone,
Trillions perished with a moan,
Now these last remnants
wage lonely battles in a brutal field:
Metallic haze, soot and dusty crumbling sky,
Outnumbered and surrounded

by the winning ever-axing army,
One after the other
they are cut, lopped, snapped and pruned,
so one after other they fall,
Every single minute
thousands of these soldiers
are cut, wounded and slaughtered,
Odds are all against them,
Even their own patron deity
—mother nature—
now turns against them,
The windstorm aids the enemy,
The cemented houses are very strong
against the nature's throng,
Almost none of them break,
Just a few poor huts shriek,
But the lonely, thin, scattered units
of the trees are fragile and weak,
Staring at a future very bleak,
They easily give in with a creak,
The howling storm eats their jarring shriek,
So they fall
with a painful call,
They are already tired
in the brutal game of survival,
They cannot fight
as a robust, harmonized army,—
a strong grove, a little fighting unit,
capable of bearing the stormy onslaught,
So the scattered soldiers fall easily
as their strength lies in groups,
absorbing the storms as an entity,
So the trees that have struggled
to survive and sustain
and luckily still endure the axe
fall and tumble to the airy push,
Weak they are and lonely,

so easily they fall down,
Just like lonely and alienated humans
caught on the island of depression
far away from the
lush green of human affection and connection
fall prey to
sickness, suicide and killing madness.

A playful birdie guy

White-browed, fan-tail flycatcher,
A big name for a little bird,
But it's a sweet, playful birdie
you ever heard,
For hunting is its play,
A lucky bird indeed
for having the survival duty
as a playful booty.

It chases the houseflies,
Dips, dives, sallies,
curves, twists, dallies,
moves, shakes and turns
for many a fabulous airy churns,—
Just a pleasant game
in survival's name,
The flies don't fly far and high,
Among them its playgrounds lie,
It chases them along
their zigzag flight with a playful throng,
Seeing it earning its bread,
as if chasing a playful thread,
mistaken may be one's eye
and take it as a cutely drunk birdie guy.

From a little distance in the yard
lucky is the bard
to watch the antics of this little hunter,—
a funny, frolicking punter.

You don't see the fly it's after,
You just marvel at the
airy hoops, loops and even somersaults,
The fly is very quick
and to catch it with a childish squeak
one has to be the master of airy display
with wings absorbed in joyful spray.

It doesn't mind your presence much,
Soothing, friendly such!
A very friendly bird
not to mind the little garden's nerd,
It's just bothered
about its playmate, the fly,
And isn't shy
to fly near and around you,
You feel the soft brush of nature's hue
as it sallies very close,
You get an easeful dose
of wellbeing and joy,
An untamed bird so near, ahoy!
An untamed bird flying so near,
So friendly and dear,
You feel good
and come out of your sad mood.

It gives me good company
in my little yard,
A few lines of nourishment
for the thirsty, hungry bard.

A perky, agile bird,

it flicks its fan-tail
before going for the airy sail,
It moves sideways even while sitting,
So much full of playful energy,
A happy, lucky guy
to have its hobby as a profession,
A rare bird that
makes hunting look like a play,
All enthusiastic, spirited and gay,
It stirs the same cords in me
whenever I look at it,
I marvel, muse and forget
the seriousness of life
among all the human strife,
How playfully it carries it survival duty
with playfulness and loopy beauty!

A flower on the burning pyre

It's fiery hot,
The sunrays burn, singe and angry lot,
Almost like a vast open oven,
Everything and everyone
getting slowly baked with fiery greed,
I know we need
this heating to survive and grow,
Futile isn't the sweat on thy brow,
Sows the seeds this heat
to enable the life beat
the open jaws of barren wastes,
and ensure that everyone tastes
cool, green vistas in times to come
where flowers smile and honeybees hum.

The trees tested and shorn of leaves,

Their spirit grieves,
But they have to pass this test
for luxuriant growth and rest
during the monsoon rains,
Forgotten when will be all pains.

Tired birds, panting beaks
among sandy airy shrieks,
They have to keep the song going,
keep the birdie boat rowing
for the sake of rainy days,
when there will be a joyful maze
of nests, hatchlings and love,—
a brush with luxuriant canopy's shove.

The land parched, cracked, rusted,
All spirits lying dusted,
With open wounds and cracks the land praying,
A piteous cattle braying,
Everything praying
with full receptivity and faith,
Lying open like a vast open bowl
with misery and soul's howl
for the sky's grace to fall
and bring succor to all
in the form of raindrops
as blessings with musical plops.

Having so submissively lain
waiting for the first rain
and dance among the fragrance of the soil,
Forgotten will be all burning toil,
The wind that burns the eyes now
will turn a soothing whisk
gyrating for cool shove
on frayed tempers and stressed brow.

I just have to wait
and not give into frustration's bait,
while even the iron railing seems to melt,
and brace up my fortitude's belt.

There is a miracle,—
a little flower in my small garden,
Singed with fire
but still smiling on the burning pyre,
While the sunrays burning
feel capable of churning
even the paint and plaster on the wall,
The sunburnt flower avoids beauty's total fall,
It presents a little bit of icing on the miracle cake,
Triumph of life on death's rake,—
a butterfly on the sunburnt flower,
a ray of hope and beauty's shower,
carrying the colors of defiance
and survival with minimum allowance,
A little chit of colors flying,
diving, fluttering and defying
the diktats of heat and inspire
life and hope in the air on fire.

That's enough for me,
Sufficient to ignite spirit's glee,
In this furnace, this miracle little
is enough to give me a tittle
above all dreary skittle and spittle,
All is well
as long as you can smell
and see a little flower
offering a butterfly its sunburnt beauty's shower
carrying the baton and the seed,
the prospect and hope's feed
for cool, luxuriant rains and loving breeze
liberate which will everything from fire's seize.

The gift by a passing cloud

Such killer June heat,
The sun greedy for a new fiery feat,
The wind doth burn,
Almost melting the fern.

A little swab of cloud
pitied life caught in smoldering shroud,
Thundered and struck a lightning note,
With its little waters it fought
a small garden's thirst and pain,
Aha, a brief spell of rain
on a sunlit noon!
An unexpected boon,
Godsent sprinkle of water on a face
withering without moisture's brace.

The cloud is very small,
But showers its waters all,
Wets a little garden and its sunburnt flowers,
Bathes them with blessing showers.

As a cloud tiny
it may not make it all rainy
for all the land
and salvage the burning sand,
But it knows its duty
to the sun-singed beauty
in the yard
of a small-time bard,
It's beautiful to see
a little drizzle among noon's full glee.

The little cloud knows
it can't thwart the fiery blows
to kill the fire,
but it can sire
optimism and raise hope
with its brief watery mope,
It drops a little message
with its brief watery passage
that I'm here for you,
Good times will come with night's dew,
And the soil
writhing with pain and on boil
dances with life
among the fiery onslaught and strife,
Comes it back to life,
Its joy one can smell
even in this burning hell.

A small journeyman cloud
makes the entire sky proud
with its brief downpour on a sunlit noon
when the heat is at its peak in June,
And a poet in his small wet garden,
Joyful over this tiny divine pardon,
Soaks in the beauty of raindrops
and forgets life's quirky flips and flops.

Moved on the cloud small
after giving its waters all,
After a thundering greeting it left
with airy dives deft.

A little game of loss and gain

The white-browed, fan-tail flycatcher,

The jerky, perky insect snatcher,
Sallies it on airy pamper,
Now seems in offbeat temper,
It sits on the terrace railing,
Perched like the court's king,
Looks down at a curious pigeon on yard's wall,
The flycatcher gives a warning call.

Very curious is the pigeon,
All spellbound by a grainy vision,
Looking on the floor below,
Its caution and alertness gone slow;
tentative and looking to make a decision
to collect some grain with precision,
But the flycatcher seems to give a warning,
Its notes already in mourning,
And when its warning tweets fail,
It sallies down to avoid a tragic tale.

It's sitting higher,
From there the situation looks dire,
A cat is behind a column to sire
a hunting chance to quench its stomach's fire,
The low-sitting pigeon cannot see
the flycatcher's warning key,
The flycatcher then does a heroic act,
Inspired by the book of birdie pact,
It sallies down
and almost lands on the pigeon with a frown,
The pigeon moves a bit
to doze the hit,
It but looks determined to pick its grain,
Focused is its brain,
For survival all this pain,
But alas all goes vain.

The pigeon lands with a flutter

to the flycatcher's disgust utter,
All effort for dear life goes down the gutter,
Pounces fast the feline cutter,
Clutter and stutter,
The hiding cat is fast,
Emerges full blast,
Flurried flutter and agonized mutter,
Soft meat cut like butter.

Trail of blood on the floor,
Angrily the flycatcher swore,
The cat scurries away with its catch,
Carrying its snatch,
It has kittens to rear,
Little dumplings dear,
Maternal instincts sheer,
I see it relaxing the next day,
Post the successful slay,
A tiny teat
shines with soft pinkish greet,
The meat turned to milk,
Wonderful recycling of life and death,
The handover of breath,—
Old bodies passing through the mesh
and change into new bodies all fresh.

The pickle seller

In this fast-paced, worried world all perplexed,
he is slow-paced and relaxed,
The elderly pickle seller;
a sweet, old tale's teller,
On Wednesdays he visits the village,
Ever so light on life's heavy grillage,
Gently pulling his bicycle,

The bell's soft tinkle,
His wooden tray,
A laidback competitor in the fray,
His jars of different pickles,—
Mango, lemon, chili, mixed tasty tickles,
Made at home with extreme care,
Now ready to serve common man's flair.

He doesn't shout;
nor does tout
like a shrewd business lout,
He just gently trills,
His voice calmly carries airy frills,
As you hear his kindly hawking notes,
Softly in air it floats
And you suddenly know Wednesday it is,
The day is his
for his mildest biz, wiz and fizz.

He must be visiting villages seven,
soaked in his tiny heaven,
on seven different days
fresh with their new rays,
A target audience small,
through summer, winter, autumn and fall,
for his business and enterprise tiny,
His looks calm and shiny,
Following his weekly rules
with his simple, honest tools,
As obedient to his particular day
as the sun with its dawns and fresh ray,
The rules are the same
for his mixtures of spices for local fame.

It might be a world of ultramodern food,
touchy tastes and culinary techniques all prude;
of home deliveries and swanky food court;

of food innovations of various sort,
But a bit of his pickle
still brings water, taste and tickle
to the disadvantaged tongues of the poor,
Such a sweet little doer!
Sometimes even the well-off
can forget the scoff
and may go for a change of taste
to enjoy something made without commercial haste.

His Wednesday visit,
Exact to the last digit,
Going from years after years
till my memory clears,
From his youth to old age,
Appears he now a hawking sage,
He fills the vacant culinary space,
with his soft biz and kind brace,
Graces he the place
left untouched by the economic disparity,
His business almost an act of charity.

He has his little sweet world
among the crookedly curled,
furled and hurled,—
this big, clamoring, clattering bazaar
spread wide and far,
He doesn't run,
he gently walks with leisure and fun,
He doesn't shout
like a greedy money-grabbing lout,
He merely whispers his hawking notes,
His existence lightly floats,
He isn't bothered at all
about factories and corporations with fancy ball,
He is happy with his portion of his room;
where calm and contentment loom;

where he prepares his pickles
for many a poor tongue's tickles,
Beyond jet-flying complexities,
he is joyful on his bicycle dexterities,
Beyond celebrity chefs and cooks
and their philosophical cooking in famed books,
He is happy with his ever-same pickles;
with the same tasty tiny trickle,
Beyond the stampede for more and more
(the grand financial lore),
he still weighs his world
in grams of pickles happily unfurled
and calculates the finances in rupees one, two
and even *paisas* without facing the blue,
His pocket carries lots of change
for that sweet-sour small exchange,
Coins and small notes
to deal with poor customers in struggling moats,
He brings big culinary delight
to many a poor heart engaged in survival fight.

He owns his Wednesday in the village
more than anyone else with his skillage,
It's his day,
Arrives he with the sun's fresh ray,
A gentle hawking walk in this hurried age,
And then goes away for the next six days.

The summer rose

Sun-singed summer rose,
I remember luscious days those
when your spring-kissed smile
rose over all hate and vile,
Thy buxom, fresh, healthy

petals laden with dew
whereupon well-fed butterflies flew,
Fragrance carrying mystical clew,
That was then
the spring was at its peak when,
Now the very air on fire,
Waters gone to sire
rain somewhere else,
While here the fiery summer yells,
Almost a drought casts barren spells.

Here you stand in June heat,
Singed, burnt with a feeble greet,
The heat can't beat
and eat
the essential core of your smile
with her fiery guile,
Though beaten, shaken and
pushed against the wall,
you still avoid the final fall
and flash the call
of your essential nature,
and behold the dim beacon
of beauty with a proud stature.

You still carry a smile feeble,
The once big stream reduced to a dribble,
But still it mans the post,
And avoids a complete, fiery roast,
Your small, dull pink, sun-lynched flowers
still hold the chance of beauty and showers
and raise a toast
with a defiant boast
for the dew-kissed autumnal nights
drenched with misty delights.

These fragile little smiles and petals

in the pit of fire
will sire
the blossoms all rosy
enjoying the climes all cozy,
They are like
the surviving columns of army,
Holding their little petalous sabers
against the fiery onslaught swarmy,
The will to survive against a total rout
with their rebellious shout,
They won't be out
till the rains reach home,
And cool nights return
after the other hemisphere's roam.

I call these the flowers in the fire,
Adamant beauty with a challenge dire,
Smile will win over fury and fire,
Another spring awaits
with its full blossomed baits.

A wounded sapling

A tiny sapling bruised, injured and bereft,
Just a centimeter left
with its sole leaf intact,
Narrated it the painful fact,
It was a storm
on a free roam,—
A careless gardening hand
digging the sand
cut the sapling small
with an offhand scythe-scrawl,
And the flowering prospects gone,
The wounded sapling with inaudible moan,

With a conscience asking for amends,
my softer side demands
some undoing of the harm,
Pay I heed to it and give a helping arm,
I wet the soil around
the wounded sapling lying aground
and carefully take out the thready root,
My effort's little fruit,—
The tiny intact root
promises someday a new shoot,
I replant it with care
in the shadow where
the scorching sun can't reach
and breach
the little wounded sapling's fight back.

Sprouts the sole leaf
after a few days of pain and grief,
A new shoot
after destiny's miserable loot.

Fight back is easy
if your pain hasn't turned you grumpy and sleazy,
And intact are your roots,—
The core values and basic attributes;
the fundamentals of one's faith;
that sublime soul's weighth,
If these aren't lost
passed as you through biting frost,
and the storms laid you bare,
Ate your well-deserved share
and cut you down
leaving you with a painful frown
and a single leaf
completely mired and lost in grief,
Even then if your root
doesn't lose faith in a new shoot,

It will draw the sap of life
even from the sharp edges of circumstantial knife,
And new shoots will sprout
with a victorious shout.

But if the root is broken
and the substratum web of your
core values is uprooted and shaken,
Then even a canopy all luxuriant
with sheen and smile brilliant
won't sustain you,
if you have to reshape a life new
after being arrowed by destiny's arrows few,
In the face of accidental throws of life
and all the uncontrollable strife
try we must
and stay just
clinging to our roots
even against bloody, blinding shoots,
Even while you groom well with swanky boots,
Never abandon you earthly roots,
Good clothes, modern styles
and much concerned about worldly hoots,
Please brother, remember your roots,
Keep it intact and in good health,
For it's the real wealth,
The cause of all the superficial shine,
The basic sustaining spine,
Spring, hop, drop, lop, mop
and reap the life's surface crop,
Change colors as much as you like,
Enjoy undulations, dips and hike,
But keep rooted
even while well suited and booted,
Never abandon your core values and faith,
Only this much this poor bard saith.

Love sutra

The shape of my love
is like water.
It will fill up
any vessel you hold...

The shape of my love

My love is like water,
It'll change, adapt, reshape
and lovingly drape
around thy teasing feminine shifts
and sometimes testing drifts
and still more enchanting, innocent trips
of your lovely, deep heart,
Filling it with light would be an art.

My love is like a river
and won't shiver
on coming across
the stones of your pain
scattered on your path,
It'll gently curve around
and caress, hug and surround
with its embracing fluidity.

It's dancing and in flow,
Carrying its joyous glow,
It knows one's heart is not a fixed cast,
Rather it's a panorama vast,
Where highs and lows give blast,
The heart is reshaping and reborn ever,
But my love, pure though, is yet clever
to go into the chambers where you need

a nourishing emotional feed.

It doesn't expect a smooth ride,
It feels your heaving tide,
But it'd enjoy a walk by your side,
It would be lovely to flop,
rise and drop
along crests and troughs of your waves,
This up and down it craves.

It'll flow like air
across your hair,
It'll be always eager to touch
with excitement much
all the colors and layers of your being.

It's enough and full
and always there with its pull,
It wants you to rise,
be free and touch all highs.

Why is it so happy to be such?
Ecstatic and joyous much,
Because now it can dance
as if in a holy trance,
It can see itself through you,
A glinting fresh drop of dew
on your petalous smile,—
an honesty beyond this world wile.

Cosmic dance... fluidity

Here, the last remains of the day;
There, a new day's first ray.
It's never about beginning or end;

Just a curve, a bend in which both blend.
Just a handover,
a mere transition,
a process,
a continuity.

Dance

O thou beautiful woman,
your charmingly feminine undulations
make me feel
the pulsation of life in my being.

Yes, undulations are a lovely part of
the feminine polarity,
It keeps that vibration
that soft rhythm
that lovely push
which defines life and living,
If not for this,
everything will be just passive
like a stone.

Your ripples across the
frozen clods in my heart
bring it back to
even more sensitivities of life.

Thanks for being present in my life,
Feel my presence in you,
For a shared dance,—
a dance the way you want it.

It's an innocent desire,
Yours is a lovely soft heart,

Just looking for affection
and a caring touch,
That's the least
a heart can desire,
I respect its innocent need
and try my best to
touch your life
as best as it's possible for me,
Of course, mine seeks the same
and you do the same for me.

A touch of desire and mischief

My heart's sandy beach
always awaits thy tidal reach
to bring it back to life;
to feel thy pleasant strife,
The lifeless grains of sand
dance with joy as you land
upon my beached self,
You caress, shove, swipe
and cuddling full and ripe,
You rearrange the boring design
mine
with love and joyous shine,
You carry the experience
of the seas far away
with its countless wavy sway
and jostle, heave your breast
lifefully on my chest,
Seeks your furtive, fickle self some rest,
A sea and seed of possibilities your breast,
You bring a noise
with an exquisite poise
that seeps through the sandy silence

and pacifies all self-inflicted violence,
The grains of my being you kiss
with your salty, effervescent lips full of bliss,
You sway
and make hay,
massaging me with your fluidity
and stormy charms,
Then you slip out of my pining arms,
Heartlessly recede and go away,
conquering and achieving the sweetest slay,
You slip far into the depths of the sea
with a naughty glee
playing with my pain and plea,
And I sit alone and forlorn,
almost in mourn,
feeling my soul's churn,
and heart's fervid burn,
waiting for your return,
to bring me again back to life
after the separation-storm's strife.

The night

Lipstick on Her dark face,—
the dusk a deep passion's trace
on a beautiful face full of grace,
Arriving like a seductress sweet
to beat the heat
with a friendly greet;
to embrace us all for rest, repose and sleep;
for many promises to keep,
Welcome o thou lovely night!
Help me in my very own fight!

Hope

There is always hope
as long as nature holds the rope
through its smile pure,
Survive we will for sure!

Spring

Flowers are abloom
beating all gloom
in springy riotous passion,—
aha mother nature's self-evolving fashion,
Snow melting on the peaks
where even solitude seeks
some company with the crest
to feel on top of this world and best,
The valleys abuzz
with fresh leaves and dreamy fuzz,
Colorful birds
like careless airy herds
spraying chirpy notes around,
A fresh green adorns the ground,
Come fella come!
Be our chum,
Jump out of dispassion and cavernous glum!

The dying leaf

A dry leaf rustles
as a youthful gust of breeze hustles,
Says the leaf
full of wisdom untainted with grief:

Dear don't feel proud
of this young, stormy shroud,
You feel that you move the world,
Thy stormy vanity funnily curled,
Drunk with age and passion whirled,
Jesting with someone like me
blown away and crumpled.
I too was once luscious green,
An exuberant teen
with new-age glean,
A prince lost in his sheen,
Realities hidden behind the screen,
and pride prancing with haughty preen,—
someone like me
nowhere to be seen.
Thought I was the entire forest
and nature's prince dearest,
Meanwhile, chuckled time
at my childish chime,
Blew it away the flowery spring ray,
And here I lay,
having spent—or wasted?—my day,
The pride and boast tossed away,
All dusted, crumbling on the way,
With whom you now play,
But listen mate,
Everyone has a date
with the inevitable fate,
So as you celebrate
with youthful gusto great,
Walk chest out, spine straight,
Look at me crumpled
and trampled,
Remember you should always
as you sashay through the maze
that a mighty storm you are not
which will burn forever hot,

You too will trip
and slip,
And helplessly lie
to die,
And look at the sky
with a remorseful sigh
for having run
with fruitless fun,
Too vain and lost
without looking at the host,—
the ever-welcoming 'Now'
always waiting with a kind bow.

The juice of life

Dry branches just fretfully shake and bow
to the wind's playful shove,
Leafy green branches gyrate and sway
and make hay
even with the pulls of stormy gale,
Their equipoise and balance never fail,
Hail be the juice of life,
The essence undaunted by death's knife,
It's playful, mischievous, swaying,
A meaningful music above neighing and braying.

Her query

She asked me,
How thou be?
And I had to flash a smile
and hide the pain's guile,
Then I reply,

I'm fine,
Drunk with life's liberating wine,
Enjoying the summer's shine.

My own love

My very own is my love,
It has nothing to do
with yours my dove,
And now when I realize this,
there is a gentle surge of bliss,
I own, accept and embrace
the soft brace
of my own love,
and welcome it,
without a bit
of expectations from the interest of my love,
my determined dove.

The beauty of a new day,
a fresh ray
makes me forget my pain
beyond expectations and gain
and makes me smile,
above jealousy and guile,
A cool morning opens,
A fresh day of karma beckons,
I take full responsibility for my love
without bothering what does my dove.

In the now

I see and be with the 'now'

with an accepting bow,
And the world changes for the better,
The clods of pain shatter,—
In my little garden a lovely bird,
A birdie jaunty guy you ever heard,
A white-browed fan-tail flycatcher,
Almost a mirth-snatcher,
It sallies like a butterfly
to catch the irksome housefly,
A beautiful bird with flirtatious loops
and friendly hoops.

Comes then a sound
above the human hound,
A solitary *sarus* crane
comes sailing through the air
with its trumpeting call sharp but fair,
I hope it hasn't got a love-fall,
giving now a pining call,
No need to stretch my brain,
It's amazing to see a *sarus* crane
and just enjoy its sight
without reason and logic's fight,
It's a symbol of fidelity and love,
The traits getting lost and going above
we humans caught in our own cleft,—
the self-eating sharp brain all deft,
But the big bird holds these aloft,
The emotions soft
in a world hard
gets a smile the unknown bard.

Unripe for love

You spurn love

and its soft, supportive shove,
You think in love you are,
but maybe you are just at war
within yourself,
And instead of love's healing rain,
you are looking for the same pain;
through habitual suffering want to attain
the same painful past and addictive gain;
just a repetition of the past,—
cries, separation, suffering of the love last.

Maybe you aren't yet ready for the healing shove;
aren't prepared to receive love,
Rather you are scared of it,
Prone to fall in the same pit,
The deep, habituated pain in you
is uncomfortable with fresh, new day's dew,
You are scared that
fresh love's warm rays
will reach where the suffering brays,
and melt it
with its divine hit.

Is it just about
the partners being wrong
among all this emotional throng?
Maybe you are unripe
and take another swipe
to clean and de-clutter the past
with nerves on end at full blast,
Maybe you are just
escaping from the rust and dust
of the broken trust,
Maybe the sweetness you think you embrace
is an effort not to face
the bitterness of the past,—
love and lust's panorama vast,

So how can you embrace
with full grace
new love's sweet grasp?
You think it's the same clasp
Maybe you aren't ready yet,
haunted by an array of if and but,
to receive love with grace,
humility, dignity and fresh face,
I just pray for you;
for a chapter anew,
I feel your pain
and wish a gentle healing rain
that melts and removes the past's stain,
Travel you well and get ripened full;
to be ready for the lovely, sweet pull,
Then receive and welcome love
at your doorstep o my dove.

The storm in the night

A furious night windstorm,
An angry dusty smash
at the back of our head,
Some poor, weak roofs gone,
Injuries, deaths bemoan,
Broken panes, trees uprooted,
poles twisted, wires mangled,
Birds killed, injured, blown away, separated,
Nests broken,
A poor family losing its mud thatch,
They cannot sleep,
nor can they weep,
They have a little way to kill the dark,
Subjugating it
and make it an ally

in cutting wood from the fallen trees,
The trees that belong to someone else,
The day would show their ownership,
So they cut through the night,
The fear, the excitement, the rebellion
—stealing—
makes them numb to their loss,—
an anesthesia;
getting high on a paltry illegality,
A bitter pill,
And a practical drill
for the young ones:
How to take small outlawed puns
in the face of miseries of life,
They cut with hard purpose and focus,
They are used to hard work,
The chop-chop sound
takes them in its sweaty grip,
The heap of stolen wood grows,
Caw then the morning crows.

They lost their humble house in the dark,
But they can be called lucky
to run out in time all plucky
and avoid injuries and death,
All of them still have their breath,
For them destiny can do only this much,
Their fate is only such,
Now they balance the loss
with the heap of wood with its profit gloss,
Then their booty they quickly carry
in order to parry
the chances of being caught,
Walk they with excitement lot,
They carry the wood to their trashed home,
Rises the wooden dome,—
the mixture of the stolen wood

with the wreckage where humble house stood,
The stolen wood and the mangled remains,
The pile-up rises above their pains,
It now doesn't look a total ruin full of loss,
Carries it now the dusty gloss
of gain in the dark;
not altogether a rout stark,
A check-dam is this little theft
across the miserable river's cut and cleft,
They have saved something for a new day;
salvaged a tiny ray,
A total loss it doesn't feel,
The battered ship is still on its keel,
This little illicit gain
helps them to forget the pain
of their busted little house
escaped when they like a mouse,
The heap of this loss and pain
is covered by their little nightly gain.

That's how the poor people live,
They just sieve
and salvage some breaths from the gutter of life,
They use the heap of their miseries and strife
in hiding their small short-cuts and stolen gains;
cover up the wreckage of pains,
They then work hard on it
and knead it well; its every bit,
to make a weird mixture,—
the dough of life and its fixture:
A mixture of hard work, sweat,
focus, tiny thefts, little cheatings to bet
against destiny's beatings and assault;
to stop it and halt
its march to swipe them away;
to keep the hungry hound at bay,
They are busy again

to concoct one more bargain;
to stand against some another storm
in the night in some new form.

Life beyond a storm

It was a terrible hailstorm,
The ice clods thudded with mad frenzy,
The rich rued car's broken glass,
The poor hadn't enough glass to lose,
But they had enough to be
beaten to junk in the open,
Their crop was trashed,
So they could feel each strike
as a stony hit,
Some farmers even thought of
calling it quits from the game of life,
Too much money to be paid
to settle the lease hold
and the entire crop in trashy fold,
Many birds also perished,
Nests, wings and eggs broken,
Trees bashed and stripped naked.

But there was a rainbow
after all this was over,
The children played with ice marbles,
And there were enough birds alive
to carry the exciting chirps of life ahead,
The rainbow, surviving birds and playing children,—
the vibrant soldiers of life
carrying the message:
Life is above such momentary interjections;
the song, the excitement, the colors
take just a little break

during such temporary lapses,
They take the center-stage again
once the storm is over.

The storms don't define life;
they just affirm the strength and resilience
of life against all momentary interjections.

Love's truth

When you are floating in love,
O my dearest dove,
You get another illusion to believe
that you are here to give
a chance to someone to live,
But that's a polished, pious mask
to accomplish a humane task:
to cover the need to take
something morally right from the fake,—
the pool of desires, needs and fears,
A smile offered to hide one's own pain and tears.

We are very-very needy
when we are ready
and run to fall in love's embrace
with full apparent grace,
The ugliness of our needy self remains hidden,
Run as we love-bidden,
We cover our pain with smile,
Paint selflessness on the needy guile,
We are looking for a hiding hole
after getting bored with journey sole,
To sneak in
and escape from the ever-chasing sin,
To run away

from the miserable self's sway.

We are a very poor dove
when we go seeking love,
But we suppose ourselves to be rich,
So much for that illusionary itch,
In youth a body we need
for desire's feed.
In the middle age
caught in the cage,
we are looking to boost our faith
in greying, weakening vitality's swathe,
We feel cheated, deleted
and defeated
by the youth's passing clouds,
Struggle we to come out
of the grey shrouds,
We look for the confirmation
of our weakened vigor and strength
from some other soul's affirmation.
In the age old,
our power and strength on hold,
Just a story already told,
Haunted by fears,
Tormented by pitiable tears,
We are seeking cushions
against falls giving broken bones,
Dream of flowers among stones
to beat the loneliness ghost
and avoid destiny's roast.

Love is a bargain sweet;
a stupendous feat;
a desire all clean and neat
in lieu of all the sweet sounding
treasures of fabled emotions abounding,
The strength of love

lies in wearing a glove
over and above
desire's naked claw
and hide flesh's flaw;
and confirm the needs and fears
as pure, pristine emotions and holy tears;
make promises of just give, give and give,
While in reality, we are merely there to live
and simply take, take and take;
an illusionary polish on surface fake.

Gone

A little clump of trees
on the margins of a village,
A last refuge for
some birds, squirrels, lizards and reptiles,
A mere dot of a forest,
A mere drop of natural green
in the artificial shine and sheen,
carrying a tiny essence of
the raw, rugged face of nature,—
playful chirps, survival game,
hunting, mating, nest-making,
dying, births—everything.

The sparrows raised
the songs of dawn and dusk,
The little hawks and coucal hunting till late,
The squirrel stole eggs,
The angry tailorbird threw abuses,
The cat too leapt for chance grabs,
The snake slithered around,
The peacock kept a stern watch,
The robins, rockchats, sparrows, flycatchers,—

the denizens of this tiny glimpse of a forest.

Lovemakings,
Births,
Deaths,
A composite life
throbbing with varied, chirpy excitement,
Then the humans again felt the need,
in pursuance of their greed,
for more land,
Arrived the clawed hand,
The mighty earthmover raged the place
with its metallic, predatory brace,
Gone was the little dot of natural grace,
Flew away the birds,
The squirrels scurried around like panicked herds,
A snake with a futile crawl
and the panicked human brawl.

It's all clear now,
The tamed space with surrender and bow,
Ready for our developmental touch
and consumerist trimming much,
Silent mornings without bird songs
and their chirpy throngs,
Stealthily settles the dusk
with sad wafting of the day's last musk,
No goodbying sparrow chorus,
A melancholy pervasive and porous.

It's all clear and finely leveled,
Showing how mankind has travelled
on the victory route
trampling innocent sapling and shoot
under his powerful, heavy boot,
The wood is taken away
without the loss of a day,

Now it's a fine plot
with economic prospect and financial shot.

A cemented, plastered building
will come up like a triumphant hill,
A stony castle of the human will,
To stand rock firm against the time,
Every single dust grain flaunting glittering dime,
But the sparrows I miss
and the musical bliss
of their morning and dusk songs,
The poet in me longs
for that tiny stage
bearing the raw lines of nature's page.

The futility of worldly love

I thought I loved you more,
But you too were sure
of your love as more pure,
The testing time but played smart cards,
and beat illusions by several yards,
With its neutral chime
wrote it its own rhyme,
Bared, naked, trimmed we stand,
No longer holding each other's hand,
Each other's faults we now weigh,
having eaten and spent the golden ray.

The inflated paradise
now cut down to paltry size,
The big, infatuated sighs
petered down to measly byes.

The card castle on the heap of lies

sobbing with painful cries
and burning sighs,—
Sweet to sour,
Heavens to teary parting hour,
We humans first make
then break,
First make love
then eagle turns the former dove;
make war
and firmly bar
the former sweetness to turn sour
and bitter every hour
for some negative excitement and fun,
What a ridiculous run,—
Just a series long
wherein little births and deaths throng,
Beginnings and endings tiny,
All these links shiny
form the final chain
between repetitive joy and pain,—
the first birth
with all mirth;
and the death last
with its mourning vast.

The exiled darkness

The developmental lark
with its growth songs and financial hark
waging a fight against the dark,
Billions of bulbs in fight
against the night
to cast away nocturnal shadows out of sight,
Now every nook corner has light.

We just want to have a day
with 24-hour ray
with our manipulative say,
But dark is the womb,
Flashes in which all this boom,
zoom
and the materialistic bloom,
Prevail it will
against all this human-centric hoot shrill,
It—the dark—transforms with a trill,
Wow what an amazing skill!
Dives it into the human heart
playing too smart,
The exiled darkness of night
keeps its fight
and throws a tart
ensnaring dart,
It stabs the human heart
with its shadowy, selfish art.

So into humans sneaks the gloom,
as they fornicate in full light and bloom,
Outside light, light and more light,
While inside us the dark ghosts fight,
Outside we turn rich,
Inside we carry a beggary itch,
Outside we seem to brightly smile,
Inside we frown with a dark guile.

Being in the womb of non-being

Aha that solitude's brace
with full grace
showered upon one's hassled self!
The fragrance of silence,

Away from the mind's violence,
Smell it,
Enjoy to the last bit,
But never forget the scent of humanity,
It has its own beauty,
The sweet-sour smell of attrition of life
against testing odds and rippling strife;
of pleasure, sighs, moan, pain;
of rainbows after the stormy rain.

The soft brace of a flower
and the divine shower
of smiles and tears
also bears
the stamp of the unwritten laws,
Nothing'd exist without humane flaws,
The heavenly bliss
and peaceful kiss
prevailing in the vales
won't have any meaning without
the strife and humanity's travails.

Silent whispers in a forest
and the noisy outpours in a bazaar
share deep roots,
Life is impregnated in deep chambers
of silence and solitude
and the mystical beatitude
somewhere far away,
It's then let loose
to seek a higher meaning
in the congested, overbrimming,
cacophonic, struggling bazaar.

Life comes out of a deep cave
to brave
all that blood, sweat, smile,

tears, love, guile
and hate
that berate
we humans,
We have to pass the test
and be our best
in the crowd
and then wear the shroud
of the eternal sleep
as undisturbed silence motherly creep
to take us deep
again into the empty womb of the last sleep.

Among the mountains

Away from all guile,
where the stones smile,
And silence sings a song
to mountain wind's gong,
With disarming translucency the sunrays
seep into the stones' heart cold,
The eagle flying so bold,
A new reality shows hitherto untold.

Morose and weary,
and the soul all teary,
I walk on the stony path
with needle sharp memories
frozen in the mind,
like the glacial ice behind,
With a cunning discretion
they slowly creep
by inches over the years,
Jarring the stones,
rubbing boulders and crags,

I want to escape
from all that breeds pain
for some soul's gain,
And the stony solitude
seems to feel my estrangement and platitude,
It embraces me,
Bares its secrets for me to see.

Furtively slide a few pebbles,
Dead grass breaks its drowsiness,
It sways
and prays,
With a resounding laughter,
the wind runs after
the stony peaks,
Bubbling and gurgling
comes a little stream from a glacier.

A huge boulder greets,
stifling a yawn,
in its clumsy, gruffy voice,
I just stand there,
My soul ready to bare
all pains and listlessness,
And look at the icy summit
standing there like a peaceful hermit,
For comfort, solace and guidance.

A little bouquet of soft treasures

A little child's soft touch
is healing much,
Almost an atonement for all
grown-ups' sins and fall.

An old person's smile
is innocence beyond all youthful guile,
It's fresh, honeyed and young,—
the beauty on a sublime, high rung.

A kind heart's gentle touch
is healing much,
It's a support strong, substantial more
than any rock-solid calculations ever bore
by a scheming mind
with its reasoning grind.

Simplicity a far better treasure
than any cosmetic make-up and showy measure.

Truth is God's representative best,
Above rituals, customs and religious fest.

Joy is soul's suitable food most
and happiness best meal for the body, the host.

Broken forever

It has been a slow burn
and a painful churn
going in the innards of my being,
The blades of those memories
—time in a vicious freeze—
now spin, whir and buzz,
unleashing in the soul a painful fuzz,
The sharp blades cut
and firmly shut
the door to any new bloom
in the heart's gloom,
They cut any new image;

hypnotized by the same visage,
They make noise
to outshout any fresh song's poise,
They unleash winds
to wipe away any new footmarks
of a walk with someone new,
They lick the dew
before a new smile
might grace the suffering pile
and admire and embrace
with grace.

You walked away
with swagger and sway;
away, away
to be happy and gay
with another heart's new ray,
And here I lay,
alone, forlorn and at bay
from all that might give a new day,
Because the rotating sharp blades
whirring in the soul's glades
shake me from inside,
I laugh and smile outside
and cry inside,
I should have known
that flowers come with thorny bemoan,
The petals and smiles are windblown,
But the thorns remain
as hooks
and nightmarish crooks,
piercing your heart
with a poisonous dart,
Keeping you anchored
in a breached, stormed lagoon,
Shines where the broken moon,
You want to escape from it,

but cannot move even a bit,
You have loved so much
and broken to extent such
that now you can't love anymore,
You just love being tossed away from safe shore,
In love you have given your all
that you love only your fall,
Now you take your pain
as a gain,
You walk in the rain
secretly holding your pain
and pass your tears
as a smile that the raindrop bears,
You are drenched with sorrow and pain
and they think it's just rain,
You are trying to manage the pain inside,
The tortuous heave of the tide,
But they think
you are roiling in joyful pink,
That you are laughing
with the soul happily surfing,
You struggle to pull out the thorn,
while your soul and spirit mourn,
The thorn hooked in your heart
which doesn't allow you to part
from the times gone,
Your soul and spirit bemoan
the dreams broken to pieces,
The hook so firmly embedded,
gone so deep
and going still deeper with a bloody creep,
The hook almost a living entity with roots
and offshoots,
It grows to be a dark forest
without any ray,
Its dark nights hold all hopes at bay,
The long dreary nights

with lonely fights,
Its shadows loom so large
as to barge
into your days
chucking out their rays,
Your days are eaten
and smile thoroughly beaten,
You are afraid of a lovely smile
and take it as another guile,
You run away
from any new cuddling sway,
You know you are broken within,
And now you can hardly be a mender
of some lovely heart
seeking your company for a new start,
Looking up to you for solace,
love and peace in your face.

On an icy mountain

Away from all guile,
where the stones smile,
And silence sings a song
to the mountain wind's gong,
With disarming translucency the sunrays seep
into the stones' heart cold and deep,
The eagle flying so bold,
With its mighty wings ruling over the air cold,
Unfolds below a new reality hitherto untold.

Morose and weary
and my soul teary,
On the stony path I walk,
looking now and then at the kingly hawk,
There are painful memories

frozen in the mind,
like the glacial ice behind,
With a cunning discretion
they creep slowly,
by inches over the years,
jarring the stones,
painfully rubbing the boulders.

I want to escape
from all that breeds pain
for some soul's gain,
And the stony solitude
feels my estrangement
and embraces me,
Bares its secrets for me to see,
Furtively slide a few stones,
Dead grass breaks its drowsiness
and sways,
prays,
With a resounding laughter
the wind rams into the pointed peaks,
Bubbling and gurgling
emerges a stream from a glacier,
A huge boulder greets,
stifling a yawn,
in its clumsy, gruffy voice,
I just stand there,
My soul ready to bare
all pains and listlessness,
and look at the icy summits looming large,
Peace sparks its mystique charge,
I open the portals of my confined being,
and allow the non-being
to enter my little egoistic hut,
the marks of the customized rut,
The untamed force charges in,
and douses the individualistic din,

It's all there to feel and see
and just be, just be.

Ashes

When all the wars will be over
silence will tentatively hover,
Nothing left to fight for,
No blood to shed more,
The remaining people few
will seek each other to rue;
looking for the long-lost human love,
peaceful dove,
and humanity's touch and smell
which long ago fell
into the dust,
got lost in civilizational rust.

They'd recall words kind
inhumanly left behind
in the mad race
to acquire a superhuman face,
Stories they'd share
and go for a solacing soul's bare,
They'd seek music in some bird still alive,
They'd hunt for beauty in some lone flower's thrive,
They would sit under a still intact tree
to spend some moments free
from wars and hate,
and try to rewrite their fate,
They'd drink water from some little stream,
and would dream
of all that the mankind lost,
which mother nature had given
for free as a kind host,

They'd then sow,
after that typical humans' row,
faith, trust, brotherhood and love
in the barren, burnt wastes
to savior again the long dead tastes,
They'd drop the love seeds
among the ashes of war and gory deeds,
The saplings they'd nourish
for a fragrant flourish,
With their repentant tears,
they'd hope that the ash bears
some saplings of humanity,
undo that will the past criminality,
They'd till their little field
with an affectionate, collaborative shield,
They'd celebrate fistfuls of yield,
It'll be a very small world again,
Beyond all the daunting, bigger bargain,
A tiny flicker of life
among death, destruction and strife,
The stories they'd share,
in a lilting tone with soul's honest bare,
how they foolishly fought and angrily brayed,
Under a lone tree's shade,
they'd tell how they childishly unmade
all that had'n so laboriously made,
They'd then worship even a single grass blade,—
the tiny survivor from nature's arcade.

The question

These questions are yours all,
And the answers that somehow fall
in your knowledge zone
are also your own explanatory moan,

The questions go out
with a seeking shout,
The answers that come home,
These're your own queries reshaped after a roam,
Your query is your mind's eye
wandering with a searching sigh,
It goes on a prowl
carrying its reaping scythe for a meaningful sprawl,
And after many an argumentative brawl,
Comes it home
after a restless roam,
Transformed now
after debates and discussions
ending in an agreeing bow,
It now fills up the space
left out when it went out to embrace
an iota of meaning for you,
The same vapors now turned dew
carrying a solacing hue,
The question was all yours,
The answer too is all yours which now assures,
Just some medium carried it on,
And simply a medium took it home,
Yours it was when it went out,
Yours it's now when it returns with triumphant shout,
Just a subtle change
in its appearance and range,—
The puzzling cloud turns crystal clear dew,
Just a shape new,
Receive it as your own,
The missing child that was once gone,
Hold it,
Cherish it
and smile
for it has travelled many a mile.

Momentary kiss of bliss

Don't ye seek permanent bliss,
for then you miss
its softest touch
on your soul bruised much,
Permanence is too big a load,
Leave it for the God,
Soft, soothing is the transient brace
with full grace
on your restless self,
A gentle song to calm down suffering yelp.

So journeyman,
soak the little gentle installment of bliss,
Allow it to kiss
your fatigued nerve,
Feel a bird's verve;
a stream's ripply wave
so beautifully brave;
a vale's beauty
performing its naturally flowing duty;
a dewdrop's pride
shining like a new bride;
a bird's free flight;
a child's unconditional delight;
the silence singing a song
in hilly seclusion for long;
godliness in a forest pristine and pure
where truth pervades all sure;
hope in someone's eyes;
a lover's sweet sighs.

These are little dollops of bliss
that arrive with a momentary kiss,
Gently hold them,
Allow them to kiss your hem,

Accept the little gem,
Imbibe their essence in you,
Then you won't rue
the absence of permanent bliss,
Allow its little representatives to kiss
your tired self
crying for help.

Loss

Oh, if not for this chatter in the mind,
I won't have been blind
to the softly caressing greeting by a flower;
autumnal breeze's cool shower;
a flowery branch's tipsy sway;
a dew glinting in the sun's ray;
a bird's chirpy pun;
another's flight for fun;
slight shift of a cloud in the sky;
a lonely heart's sad sigh;
the unsaid behind someone's words;
the silence enveloping the noisy birds;
pain hiding behind a smile;
tears lurking behind a joyous pile;
the pause shadowed by the mad race;
suffering behind an angry grimace;
the light hidden under the dust;
the imperishable under the surface rust.

Oh, if not for the chatter of this mind,
so many things won't have'n left behind,—
unsaid, unseen, unfelt,
unheard, untouched, unsmelt.

Oh, if not for this chattering mind

a treasure won't have'n left behind.

A dawn

On a vintage autumn night,
tremulous dewy stars
kiss the seasonless silence
spread over the lips of darkness,
A mysterious hand caresses
the tousled tresses of the night,
Whimsical swirls and ripples
of the passing seconds
in the vast, silent pools of darkness.

Someone's exhausted sobs
and ceaseless moans
now dive forever into the
measureless serenity
of the slumbering eternity.

The high tide of darkness
swallowed the star,
And the gloom
added to its
invisible shades to the far.

Then keen and warm light filters from
the eastern horizon,
Flits across the misty, dewy curtains,
I feel a benevolent new sun,
a new fireball
with warm blessing rays.

The mountain eagle

The mountain eagle
—a hunting, humming sophistication—
unabashedly flying in splendor and ecstasy,
Its unquenchable, well-mapped tempests
creating an airy, overwhelming firmament,
But does this fraction of neatly ordered reality
possess anything good
for the prey as well?

A little place

In the hills there is a corner little,
Peaceful, silent and still,
Motherly protects the hill
the daughterly shrine pearly,
The sun cometh early
and kisses the dew-jeweled cobwebs,
Shines upon the watery beads,
Fatherly the sun reads
all that was mysteriously written at night,
Away from all light,
With its softly reading touch
stars shine much,
The dew shines and smiles,
away-away from all guiles,
like the jewelry of bushes and grass
away-away from all commercial crass.

Herein I walk in sometimes,
Gently seeking permission to be let in,
Away from the noisy din,
And like a smiling host
it feels my weary roast,

And without boast,
the kindest host,
opens Her gates
to this little soothing place
set-up by the God's grace,—
a spontaneity free-flowing;
the existential force glowing.

The moth that burned the flame

O thou lady moth,
Holding 'this' and 'that'
in your hands both,
Accuse thou me the flame
and put all the blame
on my burning male flame.

You say,
keeping your own mischief at bay,
that I burned your wings,
How stoutly self-justification sings!
You blame
fully aflame
that you scalded your skin
in going around my fiery orbit's din.

Dear, let me share this,
Lies lie buried under your kiss
and a selfish hiss
under thy whisper soft
and the best fakery held aloft.

You complain of scalded skin;
of your loss and my win;
of your bruised wing;

of your healing touch and my sting,
But what of me?
If you could ever feel and see!
You just feel the heat
of the fire,
o thou liar,—
the fire that burns in my heart's each beat,
It was merely warmth,
as your miseries swarmth,
to melt your rigid icicles of pain,
And amazing was the gain,
You bloomed and flowed,
Your face glowed
with a fresh lovely hue,
And now thou rue
that it was a scalding, furious fire,
O thou my sweet liar,
Know this that,
my wily cat,
you pierced my heart
with your sweet poison's dart,
And drilled a hole in my flame,
putting on me all the blame.

Thou proudly walk away
with all coquettish sway,
leaving a hole in me,
which nobody can see,
A hole more fiery
than my entire flame,
And the crown of shame.

You hurl accusations
with an angry shine in your eyes,
But you should know the flame dies
hundred times with countless sighs,
For each little scald of yours

hundreds of big ones it endures.

A morning walk in a misty vale

I feel reborn,
After a dark night all forlorn,
When the sunrays come,
embracing me as a dear chum,
kissing the early morning mist,
opening the darkness' fist,
The beads of dew
lying like scattered bridal jewelry
after the conjugal night,
The remnants of mischievous bite,
Now they shine under light,
Glittering diamond is the dew,
Real gems left so few,
The air fresh and cool,
Refreshing pool,
There I go,
Birdy songs in tow,
Walk on the little path,
Feeling freshest after the solitude-bath,
Silence, peace embracing me,
Softly whispering: 'Dear, just be!
Everything is yours to see,
Walk your journey,
Sing your song,
Own your feelings,
Accept your wrongs,
Forgive those who hurt you,
Own the choice that went wrong,
See then how light you feel,
As light as this sunlit, misty veil,
Then you will just flow,

with a beautiful glow,
Walk slow
and shake hands with this little flower
beautifully burdened under dewy shower,
Smile, greet as they line up
by your almost untrodden path,
They are the loving, lauding audience
as you reach home
after that puzzling, tiring roam.'

A deal

Why do most of the
relationships fall apart
breaking many a heart?
Because a buyer fake,
reeling after the previous break,
met a simple but seller eager,
No wonder, the deal stood chances meager.

When two people meet,—
a man and a woman greet,
smile and woo each other
to take their respective fates further,—
some body's delight;
some balm for the heart in plight.

They tease and bait,
Testing their fate
to catch the coveted fish of pleasure,
or fetch gems from heart's hidden treasure,
But baiting naturally involves attraction,
A cute hypnotism and some innocent distraction,
The hook needs a tasty worm,—
a loving smile masking the angry squirm,

It's a claw disguised as food
waiting in the stream of varying mood.
It's a sweet tussle of spirit and flesh,—
an exciting mesh,
One catches and the other gets caught
after a nice extravagantly battle fought,
It's a complete play
involving dialogues, drama and plot,
The pursuit should be hot.

For her, the ignition of initial chemistry needs
a handsome knight in shiny armor with brave deeds;
capable of carrying all the colors of her dreams;
the fulfiller of all her ambitions and schemes,
While a beautiful princess she has to be
to make his flesh excited with glee;
full of promises with lips rosy and skin fair;
carrying fidelity, pleasure, care and share,
The expectations are very high
as both vie
to fit in the other's eye.

So both adorn a costume nice,
covering common skin and mundane vice,
The outfit befitting the other's brightest dreams,
almost fooling the other for personal schemes.

Comes with more fakery the man
than the woman
because he has to catch the huge whale
of her expectations of a complete man without fail,
He thus dons a glittering costume
to match the stars in her eyes and heart's bloom,
While a woman need not fake at all
beyond faint brushing of her physical thrall,
as that is all that swarms
the infatuated man's brain and thirsty arms,

Her beauty is all that is there to see,
The man is eying only that with a glee.

Thus a fake customer meets
a simple, coquettish seller who charmingly bleats,
Promising to buy the entirety of her dream,
Leaves that her in an ecstatic stream,
The deal thus gets done,
Proceeds then all fun,
Sadly, after the pleasure-run
gradually his costumes come off at seams,
She is now surrounded by her broken dreams,
The naked stranger stands affront,
Someone completely different,
Now she can hardly recognize,
hardly able to believe her eyes,
the purchaser of her dreams,
Her soul screams,
She realizes, while sense of victimization bloats,
that she'd sold herself on fake promissory notes.

The strangers then fight,
The love-flower bugged with blight,
Darkness where it was all bright,
Hopes now out of sight,
A separation they bargain now,
The proud heads with an angry, insulted bow,
Guilt, anger, accusations, justifications fly,
not leaving any space even for a smiling bye.

The broken boulder

The promises were all rosy
to make my dreamy world all cozy,
And I believed you,

Believed the blushing hue
on your face
as you whispered 'love you' in my embrace.
Believed the honesty of light
in those eyes, big, dark, deep and bright,
They looked a clam, balmy sea
for me
to swim, sunbathe and reach home
to that island bearing the love-dome.
Believed the purity of the kiss
purred that with a seductive soft hiss
on my lips
with ecstatic coquettish drips.

Promises are made to be broken,
They don't hold immortality's token,
I should have known
and must not bemoan,
You think a little vow you just broke
with a natural, frivolous stroke,
You think it to be a promise tiny
to be trampled easily for a prospect shiny,
For you it's just a dewy fragile word,
O my flirtatious, flying bird,
Or just the brittle assurance of a kiss;
merely tradable, forgettable moment of bliss,
Or a few stars in the eyes
unconcerned about streams of sad sighs.

You think these are small cuts,
beyond all emotional if and buts,
You are sure,
caught by the other lure,
that they don't amount to a big sin,
Such is fresh infatuation's din,
But dear let me tell you,
These are major cleavages and wounds blue,

It's a fracture in the dam
in whose protected pools you once swam.

Every stone has a brittle seam,
It doth scream
if you hit it there with a chisel tiny,—
unkempt promises, fake stars in the eyes shiny,
lying kisses and feigned whispers sweet
caressing the earlobes with seductive greet,
Hit the mightiest stone with these,
And its stoniness lies broken with ease,
There it lies broken and wrecked,
Its soul cracked,
An assault it'll endure
even by the head-on strike of a bull in rage pure,
But it will fall apart
by a tiny chisel's mischief tart,
The chisel hot
that knows where to strike the softest spot.

Clever are the feminine strikes,
They hit deep to their likes,
It lays bare
the entire structure to the last layer,
In contrast, the masculine blind force hits
just the surface to give a skin-bruise in little bits.

All done
and moving ahead for more fun,
And clever enough to put on me all blames,
Using the male's kitty of stereotyped flames,
Judged yourself to be the victim meek
and me the culprit with a hawkish beak,
Condemned me in your own court
using your own laws with a hammering snort;
using your own arguments and pleas;
your loyal lawyers shouting on me the sleaze,

And finally the smart verdict by your own judge,
Me to be blamed for the entire grudge.

Confidently you broke the stone
and left it scattered with its painful moan.

A new day

Masculine dark with its handsome, callused charms
melting in the arms
of soft, gauzy traces of feminine light
to conceive a morning twilight,
Give they birth then to a day bright,
Warm sunrays for
the leaves suffering frostbite,
The soft petals that
stood against the icy might
during the night,
The stars all out of sight,
Now the morning sun arrives
for a dewy delight.

I also come down from some lonely height
and open my senses
to what is their natural right.

It's lovely to see
and just be
with all that was lost
when darkness was the host,
It's an assurance to find
the same world behind
the night's curtain blind,
Walk, hop, jog and run,
Fatherly smiles the sun,

Dance on the stage till you're done,
Draw all the sweet pun
and ensure grudges are left none.

The mighty puppeteer

Love makes;
then breaks,
From the pleasure pool,
goes into a teary sea the fool,
Love, the tireless fiction writer seeking glory,
Writes it then another story,
The stage shift,
The protagonists drift,
The characters move
in full groove
with the new stage,
And pain in hearts rage
of those who are left out,
Give they nostalgic shout.

It's now a new drama and fresh game,
But the story's moral stays the same,
Love is the puppeteer pulling the strings,
Juggles, shuffles, springs
various characters from stories different,—
loving, kind, hateful, belligerent,
Old ones pushed away,
New dreams hold sway
for the arrivals fresh,
The past ones safely thrown in the trash,
They newcomers excitedly brush
against each other with reinvigorated crush,
Spins it out more stories,
They look all different for fresh glories,

But are essentially the same;
just a convenient change of name
boosted by the new crush,—
the same old emotional flush and blush.

All this while,
love first shapes with smile
then reshapes with guile
the same clay
for its titillating play,
Some tears of pain
to pay for someone's pleasure and gain,
A teary rain
goes in vain
in the eyes now turned unknown,
A sad, resigned smile
to pay for someone's new guile,
A cry
for someone's heart gone dry,
Some pieces broken
for someone's ambition's completion.

Love, the master, is never short of carriers,
Beats it all resistance and barriers,
The vast effulgent emotional sea,
Seething, boiling in many hearts with glee,
So many volunteers to bear the load
on their shoulders with glory and head bowed,
To be its prisoner is a sadistic delight,
Privileged one feels to lose logic's sight,
The royal palanquin's bearer poor,—
the tireless walker and humble doer.

And the show goes on
amidst joyful shouts and many a painful moan,
Some eyes lose their stars
that shoot off after friction and wars

and find new
fresh dew
on the flowers in fresher eyes,
The old one just sadly sighs,
Thus, the show of love goes on,
The seeds of the same old story get re-sown
for the same plot in bottles new;
from a different window the same view,
The stage is the same
with stale plot and characters lame,
but some characters heartlessly ruffled
and mindlessly shuffled.

A full moon night in a forest

The full moon with coquettish preen
smiles through a canopied, leafy screen
of the *chir*-pine forest
to light a tiny lamp
for some soul caught in depressing swamp;
to light a heart gone all dark and damp.

The crickets jingle
to mingle
with a broken dream's notes stale,
And compose songs to fill up the little dale.

The mountain wind drums,
Silence hums
a song using hardy pine needles,
An owl mischievously twiddles
the brooding shadows with its hoot,
The bushes listen; some bare, some in fruit.

Unconcerned the wind plays its song,

Unbothered of the mysterious shadows long
that throng
the looming swabs of loneliness and fear,
A curious ray catches someone's unseen tear.

The moony raylets sneak in,
filtering through the canopy with their milky din,
They grope around for earthly fun,
The shadows play with them and run,
The darkness and light play,
trying to keep each other at bay,
The wind raises a chorus
through dewy translucence and solitude porous,
It's the tune of mother nature's
unbound hilarity
unmatched in parity.

The dew-crowned wilderness, the free vagrant,
The music fragrant,
Intoxicating and alluring,
Honeyed peace pouring,
A natural brew against dark fate's bite,
A soft, fragrant heart's culinary delight,
The bushy growths looking up at the trees' height
to become a stalwart tree
and kiss someday the air all free.

There are corners where
no sunrays come kissing earth for its share,
They miss the valley's morning mist
and await the fate's favorable twist;
longing to bloom and give birth
with procreative joy and energetic girth,
The secluded corners look at the moon
for some solace and soul's boon,
The sun is too shiny and still shuns them,
The moon they can cajole, caress and kiss its hem.

The peaks around
looming with a pride unbound,
The moony beauty caresses their hard edges,
They melt and abandon their arrogant badges,
The highest of the high,
look into the night's eye,
surrender their arrogance with a palpable sigh.

The play of moon on night's dark face,
Giving each other ample space
with friendly bonhomie and grace,—
a mystical combo of white and dark;
a black eagle and white lark,
Gently creeps the milky light
into the folds of darkness without tussle and fight,
Not trying to annihilate it,
Just zestfully temper with it a bit,
So that it melts somewhat to the friendly ray
and turns to pleasant shades of gray.

A lovely transformation in a mountain forest
on this full moon night dearest,
There are hearts that can delight
in these subtle shades and forget all plight,
The day hides many things in shrewd deliberation,
which now come out for freedom and celebration,
Free from all prying eyes
and dry, dreadful sighs.

Ode to an autumnal full moon

A full moon,
shining like the sun on a joyful noon,
on this autumnal night,

What a wonderful sight!
The milky rays,
Whispers through them divinity and says,
'Sleep thou my child
after the daylong hankering wild!'
The darkness is lit,
The milky rays even sneak a bit
into my tired, resting heart,
and stroke to life some sleeping art,
creating a smile on my dreamy face,—
A glow, a hope, a new dream's trace,
Its lovely, soft fingers brace
with a caring lover's grace,
The pain gone,
after a soft mumbling and sleepy moan,
The full moon just for me shone.

The translucent nectar milky
filtering through a veil of dewy mist silky,
It assuages, alleviates the pain
born of dreams broken and efforts gone vain,
Their pieces still tightly held in my fist,—
the long list
of shattered aims, goals, ambitions and wishes,
Grasp I also the shattered love pieces
and the smell and touch of those kisses;
hold them in my grasp like gems,
The glassy shattered pieces on heart's hems,
They cut the flesh on my grasping palm,
but the heart finds this sweet pain a balm.

The night jasmine is all abloom;
all fragrant with a seductive smile in the gloom,
In little corners, defeated darkness hiding
with a predatory guile and evil tiding,
All and everything relaxed and joyful
after crossing another mile with effort soulful,

Sleeping with dreams of repeating the same
with the coming new sun's fame.

Some lone lark,
fighting its sorrowful dark,
lets loose a pining song
finding its loneliness too long,
The sadly sweet notes awaken me
and ask me to be
a witness of its melodious litigation
in the final court for some mitigation.

The full moon on a misty autumnal night,
And the lark's song of sorrowful, nostalgic bite.

Shy, scared verses

Where does my poetry surface the best
and pass my conscience's test?
Where do my emotions aren't shy to come out
and pour out with full pout and freely shout?
Where does my poetry safest feel
and enable the soul to heal?

It seeks disposable paper scraps,
Ruffled, frayed, crumpled chits of paper
no longer in usage's traps,—
an old bill of no use for financial crawl;
some shopkeeper's calculating scrawl;
some receipts time-worn;
some redundant acknowledgment-slips almost torn,
Anything that has no value anymore
to lay claim to something higher with its useful roar
than some defeated verses;
nothing to draw from their consumerist purses.

My poems, my emotions' offsprings seek
these dust-binned items meek
and cling to this papery trash
like autumnal dew clings to roses fresh,
Both are unrequired expressions of devaluation
beyond monetary gain and valuation,—
The slip of paper useless after a petty task done;
a common, rumpled, soiled run,
And my verses just lost beads
from a necklace broken by time's testing deeds,
Both are floating around to cling
to some similar worthless thing.

The scraps and chits of paper look
eager to voluntarily enter their grave's nook,
The verses avoid shiny, sleek pages
and well-bound diaries of literary sages,
or a flower-bordered, fragrant paper,
or the shiny screen of a notepad dapper,
or a computer costly,
or a precious smartphone addictive mostly,
They are afraid of them, these verses mine,
Like a beggar scared of a bungalow with palatial shine,
They seek poor quarters to conceal,
where they won't feel
the shame of their naked urge;
where they can merge
with the filth, squalor and misery of truth,
They just need poor quarters all uncouth
to hide and feel alive and safe,
They just need poor, soiled clothes of a waif
to hide their skeletal, pathetic body and shape,
They merely seek something to drape
that's of no human use,
They just ask for little bits of refuge,
Maybe they want to hide

even from their own self's tide,
They are looking for things
whereupon nobody's attention clings;
the things that are worthless more
even than the scraps in a dustbin's trashy core.

New

You came
and became
a part of me,
Became my own eyes to see
more of living and life
among all this painful strife,
Part of an enlarged me
became thee.

Time's tidings swept away
by the new ray,
Alas, set then the sun
after its daylong fun,
Joys finished after the sweet run.

Some new heart now you light,
Leaving me in darkness to fight,
And the sweetest memories out of sight.

With my broken self,
I wander with a piteous yelp,
Still, it's sweet pain,
Memories drizzle sometimes as fine rain,
Nothing goes in vain,
In first adding and then cutting me,
A new version at least I be,
Remodeled, resized, reshaped,—

Hidden scars beneath the worldly drape,
Anyway, I'm something new,
And hold my heaven in a drop of teary dew.

Broken toy

You broke me beyond repair,
each piece lying scattered in despair,
You, a child playing with a toy,
full of joy,
Then on a childish whim
suddenly went for the bud's beheading trim,
Giving it sorrows full to the brim,
Kicked it away
and moved with swagger and sway,
To make a fresh heart's hay,
Away, away!

Here the broken toy lies,
Its each cracked part separately dies,
Multiple deaths these are,
While you play again far,
with no emotional bar,
Smartly you play with another toy,
Showing marvelous ease and joy.

The broken toys aren't fit for love again,
No rainbow after the rain,
Catch they no child's fancy chain,
They just keep the memories and the past
through sad nostalgic blast
lynching their broken parts,
Gain some unprofitable arts,
And then crumble
with silent rumble

and die finally with a sigh
and a sadly smiling bye
to the child far away
playing with full heart's sway
with another toy,
All joy, all joy!

Moving on

Anger should mellow down a bit,
and melt later to turn sorrow in its little pit,
then change into forgiveness and pity,
followed by acceptance with peace in its kitty.

And maybe then friends dear,
we can afford a gentle smile with pardoning tear,
And welcome a new day;
anchor the bruised self in a safe bay,
And remember the past with nostalgia painless,
And move on with ease, all chainless.

Journeyman, that's how we ought to proceed
on our path without hate and anger's mislead.

A higher dose of love

There I walk in a little hill forest
with a sad heart cracked beyond repair,
Broken dreams and soul in despair,
Everything seems caught in futile twists;
just a pointless glimpse of shifting mists,
Big questions stare in my face,
taunting and eager to bring disgrace:

'Is it light embracing darkness and blight,
or darkness welcoming light?

Love, longing and loss
brewing pining mist among solitude and moss
in the morning woods all fresh,
away from noisy worldly clash,
I walk on a path lone;
a little trail smiling as if entirely my own,
Then the sunrays streak in,
Everything turns into love's twin,
Loss and longing glide away
with misty vapors on this lovely day,
Love is nothing but all the emotions lesser
sublimated fully; leaving no victim, no oppressor.

Ode to silence

Incomplete is each word;
just an abstract, broken fragment blurred;
a mere orphan left behind
by the eloping thoughts in the mind.
And the mind itself a fragment grainy
in the overall consciousness super-brainy,
Words are mere grains of sand,
With sand-grains we make castles on slipping land;
huge castles that we cast in chase
of the ever-missing meaning of life in the haze,
Then the sand slips
and we go for awkward flips.

Words are mere broken arrows,
With them the scope of capturing Truth narrows,
How will one even win a war
with broken arrows sprayed wide and far?

Words are mere sparks;
temporary flashes and missed marks,
They come out of the endless coffers of silence;
from creative womb untouched by strife and violence,
They just give a little flash of light
around our feet as we jostle and verbally fight;
seeking a way out of our riddles
with our prattling and childish twiddles.

Words are mere twinklings brief;
provide a momentary anchor and relief,
They sparkle on the vast canvas of silence
beyond all love-talks and linguistic violence,
They themselves tell their story
of incomplete, scattered, fragmented glory,
Convey they their emptiness own
behind all the meanings taken on loan,
And the moment we listen to their tale,
we arrive at the Truth's primordial, silent vale.

The moral of their story is silence;
emptiness behind all this tweeting violence,
As I write this,
I hear the humming of silence and its bliss,—
megh naad's rumblings deep;
the booms of clouds from pools of eternal sleep,
It buzzes and booms across my head:
a booming cosmic storm joyously mad,
It peels the outer shell of words;
crushes the stones
in the minds of bookish nerds;
then gives wings to the stone-crush
to make it fly like freest birds;
to go flying with the winds free
with a joyous, crazy, unbound spree,
The words getting sucked into a void,—
a cosmic cascade;

a whirlpool ecstatically paranoid,
And beyond that silence, stillness and emptiness,—
the 'lightness of being' beyond all heaviness.

September

Rains and more rains,
Mold in the pickle jar,
White coral mushroom on the rotting plank,
Potatoes with spikey sprouts,
Baby frogs everywhere,
Lots of nests in the trees and plants,
The sky laden with flying insects,
Well-fed serpents and croaky long-limbed toads,
Thickly overgrown trees and promiscuous creepers,
The air with a musty smell,
The railings more rusty,
The sky just a cloudy canvas,
Hot teas and spicy *pakoras*,
Smiles,
Gossips,
Love and loss in the season of moss,
Well-bathed caravan looking to sneak in
and take a shelter in the autumnal camp,
Well, it has been too damp,
Welcome now the sunny lamp.

A diet for gutsy guys

Eat all your pains yourself,
Be utmost glutinous in it,
Don't share them,
And then take long-long sips

of all the insults hurled at you,
Don't share them as well,
Believe me, fed on this cattle feed
you will emerge as a
strong, gutsy, thick-skinned human-animal.

Little stream

Little hills,
A verdant small valley,
And a curvaceous beauty,—
A stream rippling across the stones,
Its unchained notes singing a song
for the tired traveler who stops by it,
Its divine fluidity melting
the stony pain in his heart,
Its free will flowing joyfully,
setting him free from the
prison of fears, worries and tension.

Bringing life to a still-born morning

A gloomy grey dawn with shades deep,
All silence except the lonely katydid
that still kept its hopes alive for a mate
through its unhurried *breep breep*.

The sky hung spent,
Looking forlorn with languorous bent,
Discharmed after overexerting itself in
breaking September rain record,
The earth below soaked full
and lay sleepy like an overfed bull.

No rockchats for their pre-dawn birdy chatter,
Things are always supposed to be better,
Then the faint traces of a new day
filtered across the clouds with a new ray.

A handsome oriental magpie robin
took over the chorus from the tired katydid
and the dandy black and white bird's
teasing, naughty chitter broke the ice.

Instantly a couple of peacocks
took the baton and gave gruffy hoots,
A crow cawed,
A dove sent its docile notes,
A white wagtail chipped in,
A few sparrows gossiped in the branches.

The morning chorus singers
increased in variety and numbers,
It's the birds who announce
a new day with most beautiful pronounce,
Listen to their proclamation;
the chirpy exclamation,
They always seem wishing you
the best of a morning with brightest hue.

Philanthropy of a common man

I'm a common man with modest means,
and common people have to be
conscious of their deeds
that may justify
their philanthropic conscience.

They have their limitations
and need to look for small avenues
to satisfy the good spirit.

I am no exception,
I collect my tiny grains of good deeds,—
a potted rose feeling extremely thirsty;
its buds and leaves drooping dispiritedly,
I pour water with care and consideration,
Within fifteen minutes I see the results,
The branches straighten and leaves turn taut,
The buds raise their heads again,
Tomorrow they will smile fully without refrain.

Now who says that good deeds
don't sow fruitful seeds?

Synchronicity

A guava leaf
holding months of age in its sheaf;
richly yellow, thick, grand old;
ripe with age, wisdom and bold,
A fully lived life,
no longer scared of death's knife,
No longer cringing about branch's hold;
so graceful and accepting the leaf old,
It then lets go of its grip
tumbles down with a liberating flip,
It creates a soft thud on the car's roof
and lies there free, liberated and aloof.
A successful journey's end;
the closing of the musical band.

Well, I believe some stately wise old man,

having enjoyed life's fullest tan,
also died peacefully in sleep;
fully swathed in life's wrinkled folds deep;
completed a meaningful life all joyful
among grandchildren and rooms toyful,
I feel he left exactly at the same time
when the leaf fell with a wispy chime,—
aha a synchronous rhyme!

.

Crawling for a new day

The day
holding its last ray,
The dusk
at its mellifluous cusp,
The breeze stops
to welcome dew drops,
To the nest
birds return for rest,
The leech
also has to reach
a place safe,
To crawl,
cling and brawl
on a new day.

Ode to solitude

Embraced by the silence pining,
The stillness of these mute hours softly shining,
More detached grows its unattached self
beyond associative boons and collective pelf,
It stands aloof

with its bold, mischievous spoof
like the misty and dewy distance
virginally spread out with pleasant persistence
under the starlight,—
a sleepy, dewy delight.

Thus, the lone pine
felt absolutely fine.

The baggage

I carried the load of victory
and the next time
when I lined up for the run
I lagged behind like a burdened beast.

I carried the baggage of defeat
and perspiring under the load sat down,
gasping for breath,
and could just manage to see
others lining up for the run.

A story

The story told by the soul to its own corpse:
"Once I flew and frolicked high,
Now the flesh and blood gone dry,
The real me withdrew with a painful sigh,
They say, 'I was destined to die,'
It's but the biggest lie!"

The night

Too far and deep,
I have gone into the pit of gloom,
And lost in the cavernous folds
of the impending doom,
Even the brightest big suns
now appear too far,
Faint stars these now
that just flash their feebly inspiring rays,
The frail raylets reaching me
cannot take out the ship caught in treacherous bays,
I know the futility of the beckoning light,
Even in its brightest folds outside,
hope was always out of sight,
Now I go deep into my night,
With nobody as a witness to my plight,
All cherished dreams out of sight,
A wingless bird that tried to fly
but then crashed from its struggled height
with a dejected sigh,
Now I just silently walk
into the dark hold of my night,
Alone
and forlorn,
The echo of my soft moan,
carrying me into hitherto unreachable zone.

Holy fire

I am the moth
and I love my flame!
My fire!
But I feel the burning core
of the glow around which

I helplessly circle!
I know that I cannot stop
the fire from burning,
So I throw myself in a fiery pit
to forget my dear flame's burning plight!
I throw myself in a bigger fire
so that I forget myself
and my flame's cries!

The voice inside

Forget about the hoot and holler
emanating from the world outside,
And give an ear to the soft and murmurous
cooings emanating from the soul,
It has a soft and sympathetic
message for you only,—
your most personal message,
meant only for you,
Listen to these delicate chimes,
It'll help you in finding peace in chaos,
In getting a foothold in the stampede,
In feeling rest, repose and respite
against constant buffeting by the world around,
It'll help you in breaking
the hardest of superficial layers,
which suffocate and limit your identity,
And put you face to face with
your true self, your real worth,
Listen to it, close your eyes,
And pay attention with all your heart,
Just for a change,
don't look far, look closest at yourself,
It'll be as uneventful as looking

at a dust particle around your feet,
But it changes the universe for you,
You will have the biggest message
in the softest of whispering phrases,
And it'll help you in finding yourself.

Midnight musings

A few night-blossoming jasmine flowers muse with fun:
'Dewy fun under nightly sun
Swathed in the cool shades of a misty night,
We stand brave with smiles and innocent delight,
When all sleep,
we have promises of smiles to keep,
So we hold the beacon of love and light
with our softest might,
The moon is our sun,
When you will get up in the morning,
you can't imagine how much was the nightly fun!'

Sweet pangs of nostalgia

Holding a dream in my fist,
Staring at the misty past
and forcing myself not to see the future
eager to unfold itself too fast,
I wave at the nostalgic strains
still beckoning and faintly alive,
How I wish I could dive
back into the pools of the past,
To have my moments last
at a place that held me in its cradle soft,
That pious embrace which still holds me aloft!

A fatherly whisper

Parental love loops around with a new ray
on an early winter day,
The mighty lord whispers in a soft voice,
'My son grow thou strongest in spirit
and sire chances for those without any choice!'

A portrait of love

She thought she'd found an exotic bird,
All past disappointments blurred,
Love adopted a new word,
Joyfully her female self stirred,
But alas he turned out to be a nerd
deeply absorbed in black and white;
carried just a quite light,
It was no rainbow bright,
The prince of her dreams out of sight,
Again a restless night
after that free float and frolicking flight,
Vanished that fresh delight
which arrived with the repackaged love,
The bruised self coming to life with fresh shove,
It was but the same hand
in a different glove.

There she stood with her broken dreams,
Shorn of newfound themes,
Trashed were all schemes,
Dry went the rippling streams.

Back to the same self,
Again the same painful yelp.

But was it his fault
if her feminine fancy hit the vault
and soul absorbed in new exalt?
Fault wasn't on his part,
Like hers it was a similar heart
passionate about some art,
But looking for a new start,
she assumed him to be high, apart
and extremely smart.

He was just the same,
Like anyone for blame
or simple, common acclaim,
But the unmet dreams in her eyes
filled up the colors of fame
in his empty and simple canvas.

He was just a creation of her own,
A normal man put on illustrious throne,
He was no king
to whom her creation could cling
and joyfully sing
the ever-fresh love song,
And before long,
she realized something was wrong
because missing was heart's gong,
She saw the reality with sad eyes
and read many lies
that her colorful dreams had told,—
as gold stones were sold.

Whose fault is this?
Whom to blame for the miss?
Who couldn't sustain the bliss

of the fresh love's kiss?
Is it the man for being the cast,
spread where her dreams vast?
Is it the woman who cast colors her own
with her spirit all excitedly flown?

The ruler of a prison

O thou poor mankind,
A king in deluxe imprisonment,
Reveling in entanglements of prejudices,
Enjoying conventions and their privileges,
Illegalities creeping in the shadows
of name and fame,
While mother nature watching with silent fury,
the child's twisted innocence
and dominant frivolities,
His soul rusting due to routine,
The material self
moving with a firm, commanding step,
The fat hominid arrogance
smirking with malicious fullness,
Surrendered to splendid helplessness
and puerile amusement,—
A king indeed
who learnt to rule hell
after destroying all that
which was once heaven.

Far away from the maddening crowd

Far away from tiresome illusions;
the rancor and bitterness of

abundant moral rigidities;
where love's crazy preambles
push one against the other for mad passion,
leading to
loveless entanglements and relationships;
where the best plan can be
to gulp down humiliation
in a single swallow;
the dormant grief seeking exit
through illusionary pathways;
helpless, exhausted mind
ironing and re-ironing the past;
ensnared in custom's captivity;
sickened souls infested with bugs of gloom;
ruled by the confidantes of whispering shadows;
the embittered paradise
with its wreckage of social weight;
where one ought to
learn to love practically and survive;
the ghosts of guilt
soaping and cleaning the dusted conscience;
where one is always pursued
by an unknowable shadow
with its secret impulses of tenacious longing,
catching one in a blinding flash of immaturity;
where what strikes as love
is usually an assemblage of conveniences,—
name, fame, home, hearth, security and wealth;
where the mistress of fate
rules with fantasies of sin and whispers,
'You can be happy in love many times';
where the custom of normal love
is simply for routine use;
where dreams are always shifting away
from the zone of possibility.

Away from all this

wreckage of social weight,
Away from the
cuffs and collars of pretensions,
Here in this restorative solitude,
The seed of joy sprouting
from the mystery-shrouded soil,
Here I feel love without lies,
Here fears reconcile to refreshed vitality
and the soul feels pure love,—
the one primary love
that is immune to all contagions.

The cost of love

The foaming sea of memories
swashing on the
hot beach of my heart,
carrying infinite illusions
on its muleback,
Her beauty's fireworks keeping alive
the youthful torrents of love
even in a greying head.

Caught in the throbs of love and longing,
Mired in endless suffocating tedium
following the ephemeral splendor,
sumptuous ceremonies and celebrations
of the fresh dose love,
here I plod like a luckless ass
sinking into the quicksands of pain.

Aah, the barbarous vacillations of time!
My persona mined with pain
born of the love that was lost,
Misery pulling me with abominable longing,
I walk with faltering strides,

She is still there
as a mirage on the burning sands,
Smiling, drawing me further
into the barren innards of the desert,
where there is no water,
hope, flower or trees,
This is the cost
she still demands for our shared past.

Some soup of peace in a solitary bowl

Here I stand on the edge
of a stony ledge
and look into the calm vastness
filled in this small bowl
of a little valley,
There is guileless silence,
I look with enormous wonderment,
Here the knots and blots of
forbidden intimacies open up,
and twisted love becomes peace.

A little stream flows
with astounding fluidity,
The sun marveling at
its own exquisite, ripply reflection
in a little pool,
Silence and peace
hung between timidity and cordiality,
Languorous sky imbued with solemnity,
And a lone lark
keeping a solitary vigilance
over this unruffled, calm and gentility
in a little corner
far away from all

noise, wars, tantrums and fights.

Monsoons

Amid the burning sands of June,
when a *koel* sings a sweet song,
it's nothing but mother earth's
pining melody to cajole father sky
into clouds of emotions and precipitation,
He then embraces her
with his showery arms.

Big brother

Big Brother,
O thou mighty cult leader,
I'm afraid you 'rule', not 'serve',
You majestically float
above the ground realities
and cast a shadow
which clouds our minds
with downsizing rhetoric, jingoism,
ideologies and vain principles,
No wonder, we turn blind followers
and lose 'independence of thought
and spontaneity of action',
Our collective mind gets primed
for a doctored reality
where you turn the ultimate savior.

I'm not surprised that
you have an inherent distaste
for free thinkers, intellectuals,
artists and philosophers,

You just hate anyone
who doesn't fit in the
the mold of your doctored reality.

A little bit of goodness

Basically, the main recipe of the dish
involves dishonesty and fraud,
The so-called honesty
is just a tiny ingredient
used as a spice while frying.

But however bad the times are,
the table full of rogue, fake, swindled dishes
won't be serviceable
if not for those tiny sprinklers of honesty,
That's the power of honesty and goodness,
Its little molecule can carry
mountain loads of lies and deceit.

Owning the self

Here I own my entire identity;
no need to just run after
fractions of myself that are
eulogized as pathways to the ultimate.

It might be that this 'I' in me
breeds my wickedness,
But doesn't it sire
my art, writing, music and painting?

Lord's searchlight

It's a rapidly greying, gloomy world
and the Lord has to hide and peep
through a hole
—a thin sunbeam through a chink in clouds—
to spot any trace of
truth and honesty
that may be lying around.

The queen of a reverse world

I stand upright in my reverse world,
With my own shape uniquely curled
as per my own unchained ways,
Your nights are my days,
You are free to scorn or spurn
or even try to burn
my freedom wings,
O thou vain kings,
futile will be thy taming strings,
How can you tame someone whose soul sings
the songs of formless love,
Eagles, you can't hunt this dove
because when you pursue me
you have your legs where
your head ought to be.

Hope

This foggy, cold midnight says,
The next sun will have fresh rays
that will warmly gloat over the wrong shades

bitingly, filthily draped around the
beleaguered, beggared, deprived mass of flesh,
Tomorrow it just won't be mere trash!
A beginning it will be, all new and fresh!

The dying year

You salute the rising sun
and the upcoming fates,
And dump the rest
as mere names and dates.

My burdened self
on death bed (or in labor pain?) sighs,
'Dears, you forget those fallen promises
amidst these hasty byes!'

Broken twice

Broken twice,
First by her,
then by her replica,
No fault of theirs,
Just my folly
because I looked for solution
in the same problem,
I looked for the remedy to the pain
from the same stone,
Getting broken twice
is born of my choice,
I don't blame them
because that's all they can do
caught in their own pain,

So what if I got again slain.

The wheel of time

A child's sparky fascination,
Its smile radiating tenderness,
Enjoying free gifts of joy,
Holding the coins in piggy bank
bigger than any gold mine.

An adolescent's evocative showcase,
All out shimmering and sizzling,
The highly stylized teeny hoppers,
The follies of love or infatuation
sinuous, clandestine and damning.

Mad with love
the youth's audacious installations,
Ephemeral love on moonlit nights,
Rigorous and virulent in its grip
(almost sinister and vampirish),
Flamboyantly goofy, zipping and zooming,
Squealing adrenaline rush,
Frantic and fidgety,
Spectacular and grand.

Stirring, intrepid spirit of middle age
to carry the domestic yoke
amid all the social cockfighting,
Skimming over the competitive scum,
The shifting, virile nature
of the greying years
spangled with nostalgia
for the erstwhile peaks,
So much the passing time speaks.

Now on the other side of age,
The realigning of compromised reality,
The poignant reminiscences of youth,
Now surface the skin furrows uncouth,
Time's acutely roving work
etched on the skin's landscape now,
The startling storage of lifelong pursuits
now almost wreckage,
The soaring imaginations gone,
Draped in humbling eerie,
the thoughts of afterlife swarm,
Gingerly waggling nostalgic gait
seems just death's bait.

The trivializing passage of days,
Gone are the bright rays,
The world just a turbulent grey now,
Snippets of life barely chugging ahead
through a dreadfully narrow lane,
And a scowl and frown,
Or some odd chuckle,
Thus goes time bulldozing over us.

The touristy venture from
self-congratulation to self-flagellation,
Bones in disarray,
Eyes grave and serious,
A helpless witness to the shifting landscape,
An invalid clinging to convalescence dreams,
Begging for stipends and allowance
of some more drab, fruitless days,
Pleading for pennyworth of life,
Poor and miserly soul
soliciting help from the angels,
Taking it to be a paradise,—
but drudgery in dungeon it is,

Horrid apparition of death hovers above,
Aah, the subversion of life and its fraudulence!
Then the last wish,
'If nothing more, give me at least
a splendid, ceremonial grave,
Let it not be a pauper's grave
without mourners at the funeral.'

The last breath fluttering a farewell
with one final wish,
'Let there be
silk-thread embroidery in my name!'

The pilgrim

How to ease the conscience
of the burden of love?
The seductive, sweet meandering
across the rubbish labyrinth of emotions,
Was it the blazing heat of passion
or the unhurried touch of innocent love?
Whatever it was but I'm a pilgrim now
seeking peace for the soul
with a broken heart,
Purifying myself with bitter tears,
which are sometimes tears of raze.

The proven infidelity of love
giving an affliction of the soul,
With a speared heart,
the pilgrim seeking the secret code of love,
And the bleeding stones and thorns on the path,—
her inflaming proofs of disloyalty.

Thus the pilgrim goes

still holding the image of that thorny rose,
Mournfully reciting the hymns of misery,
Gathering the rotten, sour fruits
fallen from the sweet tree of love,
The wayside bushes snubbing
with perfidious, malicious sneer;
boughs crinkled with wrath
like natural brutality in her heart.

Pilgrim, where are those adolescent jaunts
and big reserves of steely character?
Thou turned out to be a soft prey,—
the stone cut by a blade of grass,
The air sighing with
disillusionment and disenchantment,
Ruined memories scattered around,
The mirrors of falsehood surround,
Her velvet, docile dove's gait
hid a haughty heart's clawy bait,
Her starry splendor
was full of devouring despondency,
Her slender courtesy
hid savage snares for masculine fantasies.

All along it was love without hope,
It made me prone to
dupe my own pride,
Now, the solitary sandy swirls of
her lovemaking resonance
wafting with exultation around,
And the pilgrim walks with
his wounded masculine pride,
shorn of light and gallantry in the eyes,
Memories echoing like horse hooves
on cobblestones in the dead of night,
striking at love's cuts and bruises.

The pilgrim lost in the pale mists of memories,
Moving like a mule
carrying saddlebag of stoicism,
All soiled with her illicit love,
the pilgrim goes seeking
the oasis of love.

The desert has its storms,
The pilgrim has his own,—
bristly and jumble of nerves;
enigmatic and conglomeration of oddities,
There I go on the pilgrimage of loss
and after long-long barren miles
I gain something,—
a sad but dignified autumnal smile
in lieu of all her sweet spring's guile.

The moorhen

The day coming to an end,
The sun with its consolatory light on the sand,
A moorhen cackles and croaks
as if mired in the swamps of pain,
And I stand there
vulnerable and taciturn,
The shadows of grief on my face,
The moth-eaten memories
searing the soul,
Was it just flaming desire
coming as real or unreal love?
Bathed in pain and grief,
In confusion and boundless need of love,
in clamor and dissonance
I create the mists of enchantment,
And in appeasement of unworthy memories,

I try to inhale smell from paper flowers.

The moorhen cackles as if
with vilest insults and provocations,
I know there is silence
hidden in its noise,—
the maternal poise
to protect its nest,
Then it stops and comes at rest,
Maybe it feels that
it's someone drenched in the rain
of pain,
With compassion and self-assurance in its eyes
it gives a last cackle and sighs.

Carnival magicians

Bitter hearts
throwing angry darts;
putting sanctifying rituals
through moralistic victuals
and convention's balm
on the slapping palm,
They are carnival magicians,
Spinning and churning out everything
from castles to pigsty and brothels
—from kings to pigs and whores—
vast is their range.

Smirking with servitude and vilification,
Seeped in innocence and perversion,
Being benevolent and harsh,
In eternal fidelity with ethics,
they bury massacres under funeral honors,
Brutal and barbarous,

but with secret astuteness
they trade the promise of everlasting love,
They can win a woman's or man's affection
and confidence
and later desire
to sire
pleasure
and be in love,
They can turn holy
even the whorehouse tears,
They can smile
hiding their rage and crudest fury,
They carry an antique rancor
in their heart's wild beating,
Even their slave plantations
pass as acts of charity,
Their loose-tongued thunderstorms
pass as sermons in kindness,
They are the sunning alligators
with a splendid lucidity of goal.

Relics from the past

She snubs, ricochets, recoils
like vintage motor's crank handle,
Her muttering is like an argument
where everyone seems right
and wrong at the same time,
When she fights with him
she seems like a sailor
raising the gangplank,
sail out and gone forever,
But she is right there
and her presence and absence
are equally heavy.

In the transparent silence
of a sheltered cove in his heart,
she bangs, blasts, booms and boos
like a militant, atheist and anarchist,
He on the other hand
is always vexed and conciliatory,
The cheerings of a youthful past
try to console him,
As he lapses into glum reflections,
the memories draw him safe
from the hiccupping scorns and storms,
He seems festively fried, cooked, boiled
by the intensity of her persistent heat,
He walks hollowly with dreary steps,
But he knows it's too late to part ways,
They have shared many decades,
With disorderly, downcast endurance
he surlily bears the nausea of life.

This is the woman I loved, he wonders,
He can't hate her
but finds her the most irritable creature,
She feels the same about him,
Now he finds her a mere
cranky, villainous peace-guzzler,
She sees him as the summary and cause
of all her disappointments in life.

The domestic air ominously infuriated,
He just draws inspiration to life
from a few cuddle-animated moments
sired by youth's pleasure-hunt,
She clings to life probably because
she still remembers her dream about a Knight,
Brooding over their morose consolations,
hard-pressed by time, the inveterate plunderer,

Bearing time's hostile, incessant onslaught,
they draw the essence of life from stale breath;
from the sweet undertone of
those initial moments of pleasure,
which were accepted as love by both.

The chameleon Casanova

In need of love too much,
he turned out such,
A benchmark of love he set,
where even the most loving woman won't bet
to raise the bar,
The nocturnal bird hunting far,
The quest for love best
putting woman after woman to test,
Lifting the drawbridge on one,
welcoming another for more fun,
Softening the brutal blow,
Searching new peaches with better glow
on a fresh face,
Leaving the old ones with teary trace,
Placing funeral wreaths on loves dead,
Their eyes seas sad,
Exploring feminine gold,
The macho spirit bold,
The digger with many affections sold,
An expert miner of love's tenderness
ready to harness
and dig their tremulous softness
with the spade of his jagged breathing
on their trusting necks,—
sublime infusion of lust and desire
into the veins of love on fire.

His love's insatiable greed
counting as prodigious feat and romantic creed,
Even in a woman's presence
he feels another's absence,
He goes with an ease no nonsense,
untouched by accusative conscience,
The enormity of bleeding wounds
and their ghastly vestiges,
or slayed feminine prestiges,
don't perturb his soul
for the nastily played role.

A victim of the frivolous impulse,
naturally ready to repulse
any sense of right or wrong,
Around him the fog of illusions throng,
With a mad craze
he handles their florid rage,
He gives a purified rebuff
to all their lamenting, teary stuff,
He has storage bins
and decorated coffins
to keep, count, bury the loves dead,
Walks with a proud head,
He is reeling with anger vile
under that seductive smile,
Below that cuddling surface grace,
he has feverish impertinence hidden on his face.

Lotus

A discards and junk pile,—
a heap of things having run their last mile;
Lying at home,
Rust and dust winning over chrome,

I take it to a dump site,
Fly there scavenging black kite,
A foul-smelling hill
giving a repulsive, obnoxious chill;
strikes you with a stunning sense shrill,
A reverse pit
for our consumerist soul's shit,
Hanky on the nose
avoid we hellish dose,
The stinking heap,—
excreta born of our growth and leap,
My junk I throw
with breath paused and tensioned brow,
Then I see him work
amid all this squalor and murk,
He works with poise and ease,
Scavenging consumer shit for meager lease,
This is the junk worker's
office, factory, firm and field
welcoming him with its tiny yield,
He looks at me with a smile,
A flower in odor vile,
He isn't ashamed or apologetic about his job
where scavenging rodents throb,
He sorts the squalor with ease,
unbothered about the dirty, repugnant squeeze,
This is the dirty pit of his karma holy,
Absorbed he is without any complex and folly,
His gentle toil
in the mucking soil,
He squeezes the muck
for some survival buck,
His bearing shows he honors it,
Doesn't cringe and complain a bit;
all unconcerned about this shit,
As I dump the waste,
He welcomes me with a smile chaste,

I forget my running haste,
Looking at his smile and honor to his task
without any frowning mask,
I feel at ease
and make him tease,
'My junk won't have much,
it's worthless such,'
No problem, he says
with a smile as if he prays,
From my pile takes a little cardboard box,
smiles like a pleased clever fox
and says thank you
with a bright, clear, clean soul's hue.